Born Under the Influence

Born Under the Influence

Poems by Andrena Zawinski

Word Poetry

Published by Word Poetry
P.O. Box 541106
Cincinnati, OH 45254-1106

ISBN: 9781625494160

Poetry Editor: Kevin Walzer
Business Editor: Lori Jareo

Visit us on the web at www.wordpoetrybooks.com

This book is dedicated to my longest and deepest loves—Jamie and Julia.

Contents

The words are maps.
I came to see the damage that was done
and the treasures that prevail....
        —Adrienne Rich

I.

...this is how I like to construct myself,
my image the image of any woman...

Born Under the Influence

A Dämmerschlaf Pantoum

I passed through the narrow hills
of my mother's hips one cold morning...
no one knows where she has been.
—from "Mother's Day," Dorianne Laux

I was born under the influence of two flowers,
the opium poppy and deadly nightshade,
head tunneling past my mother's fleshy leaves,
her wrists and ankles strapped inside a labor crib.

Through the opium poppy and deadly nightshade,
I was pulled from the womb in her Twilight Sleep,
her wrists and ankles strapped inside a labor crib,
pulled with forceps in delirium, struggling to breathe.

I was pulled from the womb in her Twilight Sleep,
her dämmerschlaf amnesia blocking the pain,
pulled with forceps in delirium, struggling to breathe,
her memory erased of me, frenzied and afraid

in her dämmerschlaf amnesia blocking the pain,
my head tunneling past her fleshy leaves,
her memory erased of me. Frenzied and afraid,
I was born under the influence of two flowers.

Another Birth Story

The father shows up at the maternity ward
at St. John's Hospital on Pittsburgh's North Side
swinging a baseball bat with a Pirate's insignia,

a mini-slugger for his son. The nurse stands
at the mother's bed cuddling the baby swaddled
in pink, their longed for firstborn, but a girl.

The father refuses to believe this child is no boy,
convinced only by a glance at a birth certificate
and peek under the diaper. The mother, dispirited,

doesn't see the girl again until months later nested
on the lap between flowers of the grandmother's apron,
lullabied by an old woman who speaks no English.

They never speak of the lost autumn and winter,
the drug-induced birth that delivered the mother
cloistered and muted by the luckless baby blues,

never speak again of the lost boy or of the girl left
to navigate a life offtrack, back crawling away
from a future they dreamed that could never be hers.

The milkman's daughter

is what he called me
as he stared at my peachy cheeks and pearly skin
while my mother placed the emptied glass bottles
into the insulated silver bin on the stoop,
carefully rolling then slipping the next
morning's order into the mouth of one
for a quart each of milk and buttermilk,
bottles she scoured to a gleam that clinked
against each other as the milkman swung off
with them in his wire basket from the doorstep
down the sidewalk to his truck.

The milkman's daughter
is what I longed to be.
I loved when the sun rose and buttermilk came,
pulled off the seal and foiled cap, ringed my finger
around chunks of yellow fat at the bottle's lip, shook
and spilled it into a glass, salted and gulped it down.
There I would set the stage for my mother to become
a redheaded woman in a Hopper painting sitting in a diner
next to a man in a dress suit waiting for a coffee refill,
tapping an unlit cigarette, her fingers stealing toward his,
note between them.

I wanted to be
the milkman's daughter,
child of a smiling Rockwellian character, neatly dressed
in pressed jacket and pants, wearing a bow tie, clean shaven
and perfumed by soap unlike my father home from work
ruddy faced with a stubble of five o'clock shadow, rumpled

and stained carrying the smell of soot and smoke in with him,
downing a bottle of beer as he watched her bend to pull
from the oven sugar cookies she would wrap in parchment
for the milkman who would rush with them to the truck,
open a bottle of milk, then sink his teeth into them.

Cinderman

Those Saturdays when he'd pull an extra shift,
I'd trail the buckled sidewalk to the shadowy
pedestrian tunnel. As he looked to catch me backing
along fences, ducking into bushes, I watched him.

Long legs sure in stride marching off to make
a month's rent, black lunchbox swaying, latch ticking
in sync with his steps in clunky steel toe boots,
he smoothed his work shirt, straightened his cap,

a young man, his worth tied to being of use,
laboring toward a whistle and a timecard
at the end of the stretch of an extra stint. Back home,
I would wait for his stories to spill through the flat:

his pal Slowpoke Pete screwing up on the line again,
a gag Bad Joke Joe told that made him laugh anyway,
Old Mack the Foreman crazy enough to get married
to the young shop secretary in these times at his age.

Like any cinderman, he'd scrub the dark from his face
and hands making a murky mess of the porcelain sink,
slump at the kitchen table with a shot of Smirnoff
where earlier he gulped down a brew of Maxwell House.

I lived in this world of a man whose muscles always ached,
who drank too much, who never could make ends meet,
lived for him to pull me onto his lap each night to nuzzle
under his arm, fall asleep in the musky scent of him,

until he'd heave me up with a grunt, trudge up the flight

of stairs, loose steps groaning under the weight
of my limp body leaden with sleep, arms and legs draped
about the curve of his hunched back, sandman in my eyes.

I remember when I was just a kid.

Do what you are going to do
and I will tell about it.—Sharon Olds

When I was just a kid, I remember being
a runner for my parents' daily numbers
penciled onto folded slips of white paper
I handed on tiptoes to the butcher bookmaker.

Afterwards, I'd pay for their Camels and Kools
with quarters fed to the vending machine
that delivered shiny penny change inside clear
and crinkly cellophane wrappers I'd tear into

to buy ribbons of Chocolate Licorice Twists
or the honey sweet crisp of Butterfingers
for the hike back along the sidewalk home.

And when my father's vodka crossed the table,
I turned escape artist and dashed off to nearby
woods, wandering hours inside the shade
and patches of sun until streetlights came on.

I even devised a disappearing act behind a bureau
and vanity, under a desk or bed, when his leather strap
slid through its loops, a raw rice mat on the floor.

Now I rub the tiny dimples of those scarred knees
and remember, wince at the welt of belt across thighs
and remember, sprawl under the shelter of pines,
dark Doves in the pocket, and remember.

Living Dolls

...A living doll, everywhere you look.
It can sew, it can cook,
It can talk, talk, talk.—Sylvia Plath

As a little girl, I never wanted any creepy
doll. No haunted puppet or voodoo doll,
not Twilight Zone's sinister Talking Tina,
no Chucky of horror fame, not even
a sideways glancing Kewpie doll waif
won tossing balls in a carny booth.

Yet they continued to arrive
on holidays and on birthdays.
Betsy Wetsy drink-and-pee in diaper,
Walking Baby in gingham and Mary Janes,
stiff dollies with oddly cheery countenances.
I wanted none of them.

Not the rosy-cheeked Southern belle
with golden ringlets and starched ruffles,
not the newest bride doll propped up
on the bed, collections of them crammed
on a bookshelf or hung high on the wall
in out-of-hand displays of crinoline and satin.

I favored the comfort of a monkey sock doll
from Rockford Reds my mother clipped,
stitched, and stuffed. As a little girl I wanted
my brother's Lionel train remote to make
the trail of cars speed, smoke, and toot along

the figure eight tracks through a tiny toy town.

As a little girl what I wanted
was an Erector Set to assemble bridges,
Lego bricks and beams for cityscapes,
Lincoln Logs for cabins and barns,
Frigidaire box castoff to turn clubhouse
with Crayolas, scissors, and tape.
I chose, over dressy dolls, to strap on
a cowgirl holster and gun with chaps and hat
to cruise the block on a cherry Schwinn
or to whiz around on slick metal skates,
key dangling like some fancy locket

from a string at my neck. I really loved
to smack the Wiffle Ball with a bat,
to shoot glass cat eyes against a wall,
to crawl around on monkey bars,
to pump the air with the wooden swing's
rattle of chains in my hands. As a little girl,
what I really wanted was to fly—
wind in my hair, imagination rocketing.

Mailbox

...I mark the pages of a mail-order catalog,
listen for passing cars. All day we watch
for the mail, some news from a distant place.
—Natasha Tretheway

Those days unfolded slowly
inside the deadening cold
of another East Coast freeze—
rolled towels stiffened by frost
stuck in weathered doorjambs,
rods of icicle ripples dripping
from windowsills, comfort found
huddling at an old space heater.

Then those drawn-out summers
sticky with sweat, bare feet stung
by pavement, racing inside to box fans
for a wash of syncopated cool, waiting
for something bigger to arrive,
by mail order—its free items
and all the things quarters taped
with address onto file cards
could bring from back-page ads
of *Screen Book, True Story, Look,* or *Life.*

The stamp collection of state flags
and foreign lands all traveled
into the mailbox. Stars fell in
with photos of Bogart and Bacall.
Hope rose on Zoltare's fortune

cards: *your search for travel*
is present within. Possibility appeared
in John Gnagy drawing challenges
of Appaloosa, Arctic Puffin, Great Dane.

And then the poems, those poems—
Lawrence Ferlinghetti sailed in
with *A Coney Island of the Mind.*
Allen Ginsberg begged, *America,*
why are your libraries full of tears?
Dylan Thomas pleaded: *Do not go*
gently into that good night.
Sylvia Plath, taking a deep breath
and listening *to the old bray*
of heart, sang out: *I am. I am. I am.*

All of them stuffed inside
a bowed box streaked by rust,
slightly unhinged coffer askew,
lid squeaking open and closed
announcing deliveries, sometimes
donning a cap of frozen snow,
other times lips parched by sun,
but always, always, waiting to be filled.

Play

Inside the herbal emporium I fret fresh tarragon and thyme
will wilt in my basket waiting for the checker to get off the phone.
Cilantro and sage added to the cache, I kill time wandering
inside a natural health magazine to a study concluding kids
who get outside in nature grow to be happier adults.

Inside paragraphs, speculative researchers are not talking
about kids like I was once roaming rustbelt working poor
stomping grounds. Not kids like me who took off all day
to run around in nearby woods, took off to escape flails
of words and worries from down-on-their-luck parents.
They are not talking about Boomer born raised on the doom
and gloom of "as the rich get richer, the poor get poorer."

They are talk talk talking about the iGen'ers with too much time
at lit up screens inside fast chats or maneuvering animated avatars
in games that chirp and buzz, no birds or bees or trees. Talk talking
about kids inside highrise jungles with rooftop parks. Talking
about parental fears of mood disorders and developmental lags
who can't find time for outdoor play. Talk talking about a need
to experience microbial diversity and chi with trees.

I step outside the magazine covers, still waiting for the checker
to be done with the phone, then drop the magazine and basket
on the counter and leave. Leave remembering what play was for me:
scattering jacks and pick-up sticks, jumping rope and hopscotching,
walking, and even running really fast and deep into the woods.

Open Skate

(at Neville Roller Drome)

Laced up tight in white leather shoe skates,
puffy pom-poms bouncing with jingling bells,
hand-in-hand we would slide on four wheels
onto the roller rink's slick wooden floor.

Short pleated skirts and satin bomber jackets
ballooning in a wind of our twists and turns,
gliding and swaying to cha-cha and doo-wop
rhythms, we could wheel all night long.

We longed to be the sassy ones whirling weekly
across our grainy TV screens in tights and helmets
as Roller Derby Bad Girls kicking and hip whipping,
jamming and sprinting, pivoting and weaving.

We kept our noses in the air during Couple's Skate,
sipping sparkling cherry cokes, our heads full
of the derby girls flying on the whir of their pack
speed, wheels rounding corners, hugging walls.

Friday nights, we were just two local girls,
waiting to break into the next Open Skate,
to stride the rink on the footwork of dancers,
on the power of hips and legs—all sass on wheels.

Temptation

The boys in Princeton haircuts
dressed in madras, khakis, and dockers
just couldn't dance, were too busy
fretting college applications.
So we went for the bad boys
in combed back pompadours
wearing crisp white t-shirts,
tight jeans, kicking hightop sneakers,
Marlboro packs rolled inside sleeves.

The bad boys were the ones
who held us oh so close
and moved in really slow
at roller rink dancelands,
always with a little something
in a flask to perfume
concession stand Coca Cola
to charge a French kiss.

Those boys didn't care much
for letter jackets or class rings.
Life was fast as Saturday night
amusement park coaster rides
or tires laying rubber, peeling out
in souped-up muscle cars
racing bridges at midnight.

They were the charmers
who kept us up into wee hours
with long and windy talk
in whispers that made mothers

wring hands and fathers
rip phone cords from sockets.

They were the boys, when we played
hooky, who would call us to sing
"My Girl" in high school locker rooms,
their microphones school payphones,
with temptation streaming in
just like sunshine on a cloudy day.

Bullets

Bullets,
their brassy caps glinting golden in the dark
ammo tray tucked under a student study desk,
more bullets in a bandolier crisscrossing the chest,
bullets maneuvered across a screen in slugs
of anger and angst, in bullet launchers, landmines
of bullets, bullets of the slain in shooting game.
Bullets,
their powder packed cartridges of panic and fear,
hollow points shattering identities, blasts
sounding in sleep, bullets of grief from a spray hate.
Bullets
that silence at windows, on lawns, on street corners,
in schoolrooms, supermarkets, factories, churches,
all turned altars of flowers, candles, placards, and prayers
while bullets
fill bank accounts of makers and regulators
dodging bullets whistling by, shells jingling in pockets
like loose change to be spent in puddles of blood.
Bullets,
their full metal jackets dug from the corpse
with a legacy of wounds, bullets that pierced flesh,
shattered bone, riddled the heart and all the wild in it,
depositing dreams to urns and coffins buried in holes in dirt,
screams smothered, breaths sealed.

I didn't want him to see me.

He's a priest. I trusted him.
—one of the one thousand Pennsylvania clergy abuse victims said.

The young priest raised the lattice confessional screen
in a soft familiar hum. I could not see his face blurred
by its mesh from the kneeler my side of the booth,
imagined him Romanesque in white clerical collar
and penitential purple stole embroidered with crosses,
but could not see him dimmed behind his shield,
didn't know he had seen me fidgeting in the pew
as I waited for the door's green light to come on.

I didn't know he had seen me mornings at masses
until he called me by name as one of his little gigglers.
I prayed "Bless me Father for I have sinned." And sinned
I had, confessing what took me to him at only fifteen
having lost my virginity the night before. He said he wanted
to see me in the rectory after housekeeping retired. I didn't
know he could see me there in the box recoiling and rolling
my eyes at this new parish pastor in pressed black cassock.

I did not want to see him, proffered a false promise
he warned if broken to a Man of God would be mortal sin.
Without penance of Hail Mary's, Our Father's,
Act of Contrition, or a "Go child and sin no more,"
dismissed with neither atonement nor absolution, I faced
damnation for a covenant broken to avoid being prey,
Polish girl from a tough neighborhood with its trinity
of smokestacks, sooty sky, sulphur spoiled air.

Striking my chest three times, as if to loosen some scarlet letter,
I headed for the doorway, signing the cross across my breast
with Mother of Sorrows holy water in a farewell to the Father,
to the Son, to the Holy Ghost. Saints Agnes and Magdalene
flanking my sides, I shoved open the weighty church doors
on their raspy groan, a parishioner in defection, wide sleeves
of dust-speckled sun raining down over them and me and where
I would never return, where he would never again see me.

This Is to Say

I want to say

it was serendipitous
at a drive-in
in the backseat
of a cherry Chevy,
gravelly speakers blaring
an actress' struggle
to render Wordsworth's
splendor in the grass
of glory in the flower

want to say

it was exhibitionism
bobbing in the water
seaside, sun blazing down
on Atlantic City kids playing
gold diggers in the sand,
parents spinning wheels
and turning over cards
at casino tables

to say

it was ever so natural
on the farmhouse back porch
wrapped in the itch
of horse blankets
with everyone else asleep,
only snorts from a herd

of whitetail deer
edging the corn field
delivering a warning

I want to say

it was simply irresistible
unwrapping the scarf,
unbuttoning the blouse,
loosening the skirt,

letting them drop in a heap

to the hungry earth
flushed by the heat of day

having waited so long,
every pore willing.

I do not want to say

it was against the will
head shoved down
into the groin,
sound turned up
muffling cries

do not want to say

the new bikini
was torn from the hips,
mouth bruised
coughing and gasping
for air, for air, for air

not to say

the deer ran off,
the corn bowed down,
husks crackled under feet
pounding ground,
the scarf tied tight
across the throat,
the blouse and skirt
lost to the maze

to say

the face was masked
in backseats, in deep waters,
in the wild fields, struggling

to breathe, to breathe,
to breathe in
the long dark night.

Summer Haibun

Summer's long light swells with bright lemons, melons, corn,
the silken thoughts, facets of sunlight cascading along waves,
run of shorebirds sweeping the horizon.

It is for young mothers jostling babies in low tide or for dozing
on the soft lull of water lapping the shore beneath an untamed
sky feathered in oncoming sunset.

This time of day curtains billow at windows in soft light, sun
squints in above a rippling bay as summer knocks at the door
and we answer.

> the wail of seagulls
> wing in wild above a catch
> eyes fixed past us

O Brother,

a lament

the day I learned   my brother died
was told he was too weak to lift a phone
to say goodbye   to say I love you
from his deathbed fist clenched to heart

I thought of all the words I meant to say
miss   wish   why   wonder   regret

reasoned we sailed   different waters
lacking a paddle of words   to carry us
to each other's   distanced shores
miss   wish   why   wonder   regret

looked back   at the towheaded boy
myself in cowgirl garb   on three wheels
sailing the blocks   past cold water flats
orthodox chants   corner bars   brawls

schoolhouse halls   where we would
grin and wink. as morning doors closed
on his 1-2-3's a-b-c's   and my rhymes
miss   wish   why   wonder   regret

the day I learned   my brother died
I did not cry   and would not speak
to him   to god   to guardian angels
we believed wrapped   wings round us

left to grieve   grief a ragged companion

no comfort at my side   O brother
O brother   of primordial dust
miss   wish   why   wonder   regret

O brother
          O brother

The Blue Suitcase

The blue Samsonite never traveled
north to Montreal, south to Florida Keys,
just lodged inside a rusty tin cabinet
in a South Side Flats basement gathering
dust and must of so many forgotten years.

On top a starched linen tablecloth
and doilies she cross-stitched
with crewel flowers and pineapple bursts
inscribed "Helen made this,1968"
for her girl's hope chest graduation gift.

Inside clippings from *The Pittsburgh Press*
on her husband's mistaken identity as thief
and the governor's pardon in fancy scroll.
Others of some kidnapped blue-eyed lovechild
dead ringer for her own curly towheaded son.

All of it there with her grandson's SAT scores
for colleges he would never attend stowed beneath
greeting cards embossed in Mother's Day carnations,
flurries of Christmas poinsettias, get well daffodils,
carefully bundled and tied in satin ribbon.

Wrapped inside a child's embroidered handkerchief
a cracked prayer book, Holy Communion rosary beads.
magazine article of Liberty Avenue women's crusades
through the pornography district trying to take back
the night and the streets, her daughter at the lead.

At the bottom an afghan she crocheted, arthritis

wrenching her fingers, the one the paramedic used
to cover her, drawing it up tenderly over her face
in its carnival of color the day she laid sprawled
pasty white and dead on her living room floor.

Objects left behind inside a tattered blue suitcase
in a damp basement's rusty cabinet. Left behind
with the sting of memory, with the stilled throb
of a wound, with the body gone underground,
those things, their abandonment, the silencing.

San Francisco Haibun in Fire Season

Like some Fata Morgana the San Francisco skyline rises
through morning fog, its regal optic white spires flanked
by waves of watercolor hills and feathered clouds.

Above, distant Saturn's icy moon spews saltwater
plumes from its icy crust, but here there is the smoke
and haze of wildfires in on a wind shift.

> cool jazz on the radio
> we cover our faces
> in cloaked surrender

Anchorless in the Light

And in that vale of light/the city drifts/anchorless upon the ocean
—Lawrence Ferlinghetti

It starts this way each morning—house wrens
flirting potato vines, spray of sea on sand,
then the crows and their warnings, mornings
dewy under sun. Come step onto the porch with me,

the view no longer blocked by the diseased pine.
We have this gift of water beyond the marina,
its rocky channel gateway to a smooth bay.
Listen with me to buoys sing with wind in the fog,

old tug announcing its entry against the bark of a seal,
swoop of pelican wings. I cannot resist lingering here
in this veil of white light blinding with beauty,
reminding to hold onto this, hold it close and dear

as I was once stuck inside glass and brick, sight set
on neighboring city decks, their hubbub, drunken songs
brouhaha, all of it weedy with ivy, bats circling chimneys,
unlike these distant hills yet to be peopled. But last night

I dreamed their mounds became an unlit stretch of halls,
splintered doors on every wall, dust motes flecking air
over a muddy cliff where nothing stirred, except a parade
of my dead who nodded, waved, winked, then dissipated,

my heart pounding, but here in this new day I can moor
and watch with steadied breath the rise of light. Come here.

I want you at my side, want you to look and listen with me
to the lilt of a mourning dove's coo, anchorless in the light.

Self-portrait, out of focus

at Hotel Le Saint-Yves, Le Tréport, Normandy

I was far outside the frame, beyond the pale,
lost in the margins, smudged.—Maggie Anderson

Legs spread beneath a garden party of a dress,
at the armoire's mirror I tap the shutter button
for a self-portrait. You doze off inside wide wings
of sleep, our Bordeaux, baguette, Boursin
on the bowed windowsill, sky freckled with late light.

Here other women once waved white kerchiefs
at soldiers leaving alabaster shores of Normandy
for places far from here where we have dug in
to listen to the roll of surf, terns all whoop and wail.

In this snapshot, this is how I like to construct myself,
my image the image of any woman in a hotel room
watching wind skip along the emptied beach, listening
for the last milk train coming in on a whistle and grind.

Self-portrait caught where craggy cliffs of the Atlantic
hunch over the channel and coast, the flash of camera
reflected back in a blur, where I wrap myself inside
the fluff and frill of hotel bedclothes, drift off with you,
undisturbed, embraced by the long arms of dream.

Dancing Zuihitsu

The lone baleen circles and circles, water sprite at home
in the lagoon off the bay, having lost her way North.
So thin, so weak, her knob head rising every minute
for a gulp of air.

I stand waiting for her breach, for fins to slap the surface
sheen, for a burst of blowhole spray. I am afraid she may
beach, join other ghosts hugging the breast of the coast,
language of grief upon me even before the loss.

I daydream dancing at water's edge, feet slippered in sand,
balancing en pointe between sea and sky, ocean spray
joining in on the buoy's song.

The sun is about to set itself down as day begins to blur
and the moon pokes its nose through scattering clouds.

A train sounds its horn across the distant square. A car alarm
goes unheeded at the curb. Rippling waves lap the shore, lick
the weathered dock. The whale rises again and again,
slaps, sprays, circles again and again.

Butterflies flirt milkweed. Honey bees buzz poppies.
Their wings, their perpetual evanescence, a performance
in pirouettes skittering offstage behind drawn curtains
ballooning in day's last breath of wind.

Femicide

on International Day of Elimination of Violence Against Women

They marched in Chile,
red hands painted across their mouths.
They covered their mouths
with purple hands in Argentina.

They dressed in black in Uruguay,
raised signs bearing murdered women's names.
They placed red shoes on the ground
for all the victims in Belgium.

They hung stuffed animals in Honduras
from clotheslines memorializing the dead.
They laid under sheets in Panama,
toes tagged: *soy tu novia, soy tu mamá*

They wrote *Stop 138* on spread palms in France
for those killed by their partners this year.
They lit up in a blaze of red lights
the Palazzo Madama in Italy.

They marched in Spain carrying crosses
for women murdered by men who loved them.
They clashed in Turkey with riot police,
their batons and their mace.

They chanted everywhere: *freedom, peace, justice.*

All the Ways I Do Not Wish to Die

Not alone, sprawled out on the floor
like my mother, woozy enough to slip
and hit her head on a coal bucket
doorstop after a stay in a hospital
she said would be her last and was.

Not so weak in bed like my brother,
too exhausted to pick up the phone
to tell me he loved me, papers signed
to have life support removed. Not alone

in the bathroom like my father,
who survived wanderlust,
brain surgery, electroshock therapy,
but not throwing up into a toilet
clutching his chest.

Not coughing and choking
like my hard-hatted grandfathers,
lungs closing inside mines and mills
so children and grandchildren
could breathe fresh air.

Not from a stray road rage bullet
or gang initiation or sniping revenge
discharging a forlorn childhood
on targets at movies, ballgames,
concerts, schools, grocery stores.

Not mysteriously like the Chilean poet,
his soul sparring from the ground

against exhumation for historical
curiosity, in his eye sockets
tango dancers in a final soltada.

Not burning at the stake like ancestral
sister witches, high on lysergic acid
in rye, dancing wild in Saint Anthony's
fire under Salem's unrepentant sky
bleeding down on their screams.

Not alone, the way it is, the way it must be,
in a *world that is a beautiful place
to be born into*, if you don't mind
the smiling mortician at the door.

And when death knocks there, I plan
to stand and declare: *all my life I was a bride
married to amazement. I was the bridegroom
taking the world into my arms.*

She, the queen bee marries winter

Cento for Sylvia Plath from *Colossus* and *Ariel*

The forgetful surf creaming on those ledges,
each wave-tip glitters like a knife.

> Gulls mulled in the greenest light
> face the bald-faced sun
> with their gifts to a difficult borning.
> Clear vowels rising like balloons:

> I shall be good as new, love, love my season.
> Will you marry it, marry it, marry it?
> I eat men like air that kill, that kill, that kill.
> The queen bee marries the winter of your year.

Eye, the cauldron of mourning,
starless and fatherless, a dark water

> asks nothing of life,
> of the profane grail, the dreaming skull,
> the mausoleum, the wax house.
> The box is only temporary.

II.

embracing each other, trying
to hold the world together...

She, the one you call sister

Cento for Adrienne Rich

Wear the weight of equinoctial evening,
autumn torture the old signs—

a cracked wall in the garden,
all night eating the heart out.

Underneath my lid another eye has opened.
She is the one you call sister.

Night life. Letters, journals, bourbon,
the stars will come out over and over—

a clear night if the mind were clear,
you there with your gazing eyes,

a dark woman, head bent, listening for something
at the oak table under the ceiling fan.

This woman the heart of the matter,
little as I knew you I know you.

The I you know isn't me you said.
It's not new this condition, just for awhile.

At Pine Cove

After trailing the wooded misty path
to the cove, feet sliding downhill on wet sand,
after watching abalone poachers rise
in wetsuits from waters with their sea troves,
we brave the climb back steadying ourselves
on thick branches and each other's arms.

Back to the inn's rickety writing table,
a pot of market soup-of-the-day waiting
to be warmed, wedge of peppered cheese
and crusty baguette on the cutting board
with tawny port picked up on the way in along
ribboning S-curves that carried us here.

We slip into our oversized cable knits,
sale priced at the local mercantile, settle into
the blustery night opening a door to the sky
warning storm where we remain inside
safe and dry. Just two women getting ready
for dinner in old lodging near the sea,

soon to float off into sleep, wrapped in a sash
of fog and warmth of each other, old dog
at the feet snoring under the table where a vase
hugs three stems of Stargazers, their musky heads
tilted the way women stop to talk on coastal trails,
ears of the cove listening in.

Dreaming Zuihitsu

I dream of a room I once occupied seaside, early light
spilling through an open window, bright geraniums stretching
at the sill, voices bouncing off each other in a foreign tongue.
I wake wondering where I have been, where I am going.

In another my bike has no gears or brakes, slides sideways
across a highway of waves towards drifts of golden dunes.
Alone, short of breath, my cattail legs ache as I rouse.

In this other I hop rabbitlike along a road berm unaware
of where I am, leap into flight with ears transformed wings,
sail above a pasture of cattle flashing wide and toothy grins.

In yet another, disembodied without destination, I fly again.
My mother, wraith in the fog, waits below a hazy streetlamp
tapping her wristwatch. She calls out to me to come home.

I dream on, trail the snow-laden train tracks in floppy mukluks.
Winds hum like sawmills. Sky booms in a fell of trees. I gather
from the ground an arrowhead, sprig of spruce, a baby's shoe.

In night's last romp, the moon is a pendant at the breast of sky.
I cup a spray of stars and throw a villanelle, tiptoe in and out
of lines, hiccuping as I repeat myself, repeat myself,
wake wondering where I have been, where I am going.

Driving from Pescadero

fog blankets the road
lighthouse signals a warning
dunes and grasses blur

leggy coastal pines
bend beneath the weight of wind
falcon on the wire

Things That Come and Go

Wash of sea foam at low tide,
wind kicking in on a drift of waves.

Message in a bottle bobbing
about imaginary shores.

Sunny side of leafy trees
swathed by wings of shade.

Bee buzzing flower blossoms,
petals in the sidewalk cracks.

Canary's song longing
for flight toward the sun.

Stars flickering the night sky,
earthshine of a crescent moon.

First breath, first kiss, first love,
lasting only as long as they exist.

Coming to these things that go,
moths to flames.

Dreamers

A woman races dusty rows,
deposits bundles of butter lettuce
from the bowls of her arms
into white plastic bins roadside.

Past the burn scar scorched
into the horizon in the thick air
of another fire season,
a small breath of wind kisses

her face silkened by sweat,
cooling down her body
as temples pulse, nose burns,
throat tightens at day's end

with the ache of the field
pulsing every muscle
as crows eye new seeds
in furrows thirsting for water.

At home her little girl waits
at the open window, elbows
on the sill, hands cupping chin,
her wide eyes pitched upwards

past a cresting sun toward sky
about to darken then fill
the page of night she reads
as stars full of wishes and dreams.

Meditation at the Dunes of Asilomar

In all the things of nature, there is something of the marvelous.
—Aristotle

Trumpets of desert sand verbena
and leafy coastal sagewort nestle in

with paintbrush and seaside daisies,
ageless blooms at home in the dunes

inside the whip of wind and weight of fog,
facing the rocky cove's icy tides and surf.

Beneath a sky a spray of constellations,
lovers pass by, nestling into each other,

their windswept laughter the night's song
drifting past plumes of pampas grass.

Triolet for the Return of Spring

So much to love about it,
the again again again of it,
the breeze on fountain grass seaside.
So much to love about it,
the riots of wildflowers, return of green,
the singing birds, the simple daily beat.
So much to love about it,
the again again again of it.

She, the one who is my songbird

(a Cherita)

You are mi pajarilla,

the voice that wings the open roads
above palms and pines and hills.

You are that song
in my head,
the one that just won't quit.

You are mi amor, querida mia,

mi cantadora, the swing
and fast step of joropo and cumbia.

You are my slap and clap and yip
as you sing and strum.
Para toda la vida tu eres, you are.

Sonnet Spooning

I taught my love to spoon, not in bed, thigh
to thigh, belly against back, no feet
layered one upon the other nor arm
ribboning waist, but with tablespoons,

"Allons Danser" on the radio, two
spoons pulled from their huddle in a drawer
to bang against each other, held real loose,
ends balanced between thumb and forefinger.

I taught my love to slap the leg and palm
to make spoons bounce and click and clang and clap
in an idiophonic percussion
of Cajun sound beyond scooping gumbo.

Next we will work the steel washboard rhythm
with pop can rings. Allons danser! Let's spoon.

Landay for the Woman on the Floor

Looming large over a hundred years
in brick and mortar, around the corner stood that house,

the one just across from the long weeds
skirting the railroad tracks in the flats. And in that house

was a woman, oak door swung wide open,
sunlight catching strands of her silver hair, jewel-eyed,

staring at me and my dog walking by.
Then in a sudden urgency she would belly crawl

closer to the splintered threshold,
using her thick forearms to lug her body along

the worn planked floor. She never spoke,
only stared up at us. I never spoke, never

could once muster the words: "How are you?"
"Can I help you?" "What do you need?" Empty questions

like promises would not be offered
to the woman on the floor rubbing her ashen face

with calloused palms in the routine of days
crawling on her stomach across the boards to the door,

she so resolute in memory
and my persistent wondering: "Who opens that door?"

The Way It Is

She staunchly insists her single hospital bed
in the shared room with drawn blue curtain
is a wing of her private and sprawling apartment,
kindly offers to have lunch staff heat something up
at what she introduces as the spa she now owns.
She won't allow the television or the radio
that distracts from her invisible manuscript.
She sits in dimming light in an eclipsing eve,
wanes small and thin. This is what it has become.

She vows, in yet another delusional bloom,
to incorporate tai chi into her yoga practice
while she is able only to stand then wobble
and drop into the wheelchair she is too weak
to roll. She demands her lipstick, stolen clothes
she squirreled away under the table ferreting
the latest escape route, demands the passport
she needs to fly off in this phantasmagoria,
longing a gnawing hunger. This is the way it goes.

Under night's fading clouds, meteors shower
across stroked occipital and parietal lobes.
She wades through a trough of fog, confused
by the distance between herself and the world.
Jupiter kisses Juno. Venus births Cupid. Mars,
at odds with everyone and noisy, keeps her awake
under the same sky that holds the rest of us
silent and still, eyes aflutter with spirits of dream
as we float off to sleep. This is the way it is.

Imperfect Contrition

Under the influence of my mother's martyrdom
working nights at a factory, the husband's drinking,
her whiny boy and sassy girl, I—having adored
Jennifer Jones' Academy Award rapture
in "The Song of Bernadette" exaltation of long
suffering romanticized doing penance for sins of others—
I sought retreat at kneelers of Mother of Sorrows Church.

Decades later, at Christ of Light Cathedral on Mother's Day,
killing time before heading out to bet on the horses
at Golden Gate Fields, my girlfriend's Jewish mother
choked back a gasp when I flashed a gift shop prayer card
of Saint Clare, put my finger to the lacquered face,
pulled it back making the sound of a sizzle and said:
"Hot—who doesn't love a pretty nun?"

Back in the pew and back to my Catholic girlhood,
I recited for her a good Act of Contrition before she knelt
at the altar for the Sacrament of Communion. This woman
who joined a neighborhood Baptist church, who collected icons
from Santeria to Taoism, who received Lutheran last rites
before surrendering finally to night's deep sleep, this woman
who kept herself covered, sheepish grin on her face.

Broken Pitcher

after the Bouguereau at San Francisco Legion of Honor

At the Moscow Tbilisi Bakery, we eat
potato and cabbage piroshki, sip black tea,
save poppyseed and cherry rolls for a picnic
on the lawn outside the local art museum.

Inside, gallery walls house wedding violas,
half-naked nymphs, the elite trussed up
in lace cuffs and fur trimmed waistcoats.
Patrons don headsets, nod, take note.

We make our way to Bouguereau's doe-eyed
peasant girl, broken green pitcher at her feet,
art of the virgin's lost innocence, her innocence
torn from her. Vessel spilled,

she languishes barefoot at the well, fingers
laced in prayer to implore her Montparnasse
god of oil and wine and paint and canvas
for release, captive there with brooding heart.

Outside, we spread our picnic across waves
of scarves, turn our backs to columns and walls,
ghost of a girl joining clouds the westerly wind
washes clear from its fractured sky.

Wounds That Bleed Inside

There is no difference between being raped
And being pushed down a flight of cement steps
Except that the wounds also bleed inside.—Marge Piercy

I have survived being raped
    and did not become frigid
    or impotent or a manhater
    tethered to shame and guilt.
I have managed to pull away from hands
    grabbing at my breasts
    after an early morning art class
    and did not stop drawing.
I have slapped them
    moving up my skirt
    in the student union
    and still drank my coffee.
I have survived them all,
    the dancer who held me too close
    with his manhood pushing hard
    into my thigh in a slow grind.
I even survived
    scaffolding whistles and catcalls,
    frotteur on the rush hour train,
    peeper at the bedroom window,
but I have not survived
    the wounds that bleed inside,
    fear walking a forest trail alone
    or along a neighborhood beach
    or into some hotel elevator
    or a knock at the door late at night.

I have not survived
a man turning his body
weapon against me.

Column of Strength Comfort Station

(after the sculpture by Stephen Whyte)

...At last, at last/To rise again/Yellow woman/Moon chanter/
Truth sayer/Wisdom woman...—Genny Lim

Children squeal and spin
on playground swings and slides
in San Francisco's St. Mary's Square.
A yellow woman stands somber
between four statues
while wandering tourists
stop and talk at the Comfort Women's
bronze Column of Strength.

    The wisdom woman drapes a lei
    of purple plumeria around
    the lone one's neck, facing
    three others on a pedestal
    of rough patina.

    She slides a white rose bouquet
    between their feet, in the garden
    of glass and steel, crows
    fluttering faceless figures,
    the looming moon chanters
    lining a financial tower's ledge.

Four bronze figures stand
strong in a small square
comfort station surviving
the long memory of a labor corps'

sexual servitude.

No bullets or bombs,
no sake slamming tabletops,
just the frame of the city
around women who were
like thousands of women taken,
herded in the streets, kidnapped
from their homes, purchased
as indentured servants, dragged
into cars by men in uniform, duped
instead enslaved
in Imperial Army brothels.
      The old woman strokes
      the Chinese girl's braids, touches
      the Korean girl's school uniform,
      pats the Filipina's headscarf
      as tourists continue to wander
      in and out, snap photographs,

children still squealing,
laughing and running in circles
around Kim Hak-sun,
the truth sayer woman,
at last, at last to rise again,
her eyes forever steadied
and fixed on all of them.

Ravensbrück Pantoum

...I am grief. I am the tongue of war...—Andrei Voznesensky

Women arrived in the night tasting salt on the wind,
felt sand underfoot at the edge of the lake,
the crimes and the courage of victims
surrounded by forest and hidden from view.

They felt sand underfoot at the edge of the lake.
130,000 women passed through Ravensbrück's gates,
surrounded by forest and hidden from view
as communists, resisters, gypsies, down-and-outs.

130,000 women passed through Ravensbrück's gates
beaten, starved, forced into brothels, worked to death
as communists, resisters, gypsies, the down-and-outs
poisoned, gassed, burned in ovens and on bonfires.

Beaten, starved, forced into brothels, worked to death,
the missing women, their ashes thrown into the lake,
were poisoned, gassed, burned in ovens and on bonfires,
flowers now left at ovens, roses scattered at water's edge.

The missing women, their ashes thrown into the lake
where summer visitors row boats across, blind to ashes
and flowers left at ovens, roses scattered at water's edge,
ashes settled at the bottom, breeze blowing petals across water.

Summer visitors row boats across the lake, blind to ashes,
blind to the crimes against women and the courage of victims,
ashes settled at the bottom, breeze blowing petals across water
for women who arrived at night tasting salt on the wind.

Crossing Boundaries

We tipped wine glasses to Paris, Bastille Day,
whirled and twirled each other across the walk,
swung into the street—two women travelers ·
smiling and laughing until the hems of our skirts
were singed by firecrackers tossed at our feet
by men demanding dances we would not give.

Women in hijabs pulled us into a cloistered corner
of sisters inside La Belle Equipe, encircled us,
showed us how to position hands, extend arms
as if to shove away looming shadows
of their guardians and husbands—crossing
boundaries of difference for what we share

and where years later extremists with Kalashnikovs
would spray bullets into crowds along that same
Rue de Charonne, its sidewalk turned altar
of flowers, candles, sentiments, and tears—
women embracing each other, trying to hold
the world together, bound in courage and fear.

3's a Crowd

He slams a bargain bouquet onto the checkout
conveyor belt, broadcasts it's the third time
this month she kicked him out,

this urban cowboy with anchor beard and stetson
leaning into the woman in front of him, muttering
just because he left his ring behind last night.

Fourth deep in line, her arms brimming with a diet
plan in celery, carrots, kale, Lucky Supermarket's
"3's a Crowd" banner flags above heads,

she scans the scandal rag rack for the latest celebrity
downward spirals, Hollywood's worst boozers,
wives laying down laws,

hoping for a new line to open. Then those Snickers,
threaten her fitness pledge as he stretches past her
for a Coke and Mentos, his nearly spent blooms

nuzzling her produce, asks what she thinks about jealousy.
She announces she is no Dear Abby of the Checkout,
eyes his sad bouquet, advises he go for Godivas and Mum.

He flips through *Cosmos*' "Ten Sexy Tips for Bedroom Bliss."
On the way home, her sister Rosie phones whining
that her latest boyfriend, the one with the live-aboard sloop,

was out all night, star-studded promise ring left behind
in the soap dish, swears his roses won't fix this, not even

dancing barefoot onboard his *Bronco's* slick deck

with her cowboy with a sailboat, then cuts the connection
as he lets himself into the apartment, roses in hand,
neon clearance tag still affixed to cellophane.

She plunges them headfirst down the Insinkerator, petals flying
against her flushed cheeks, shoves him out the door, yelling:
"The third and last time," jamming a chair under the knob.

Digging through her cedar hope chest turned junk drawer,
she swaddles herself inside her Grandma's crazy quilt
made to celebrate graduations, weddings, and births.

Breathing in the long woody scent
fixed in it, she flops onto the bed, thinking
three times really is a charm,

the crack and smack of thorny roses still
spinning inside the disposal drain, the whir of them
a deliriously wild and final beautiful noise.

I've got my finger on the trigger, too.

(in conversation with Jan Beatty's "Shooter")

I've got my finger on the trigger.
I'm taking aim
at the teen stalker who left unwrapped Trojans
for my mother to find in my Sherpa pockets /
taking aim
at the old boyfriend who dumped Guinness on my head
in a bar in the middle of winter and stole my peacoat.

I'm looking down the barrel
at a rock band all-star who shoved himself into me
then zipping up said this was about winning and he won /
looking down the barrel
at my ex-husband who grabbed me from behind
at lunch time then blamed me he fell asleep at his job.

I'm staring through the crosshair
at the cop who wanted to trade a bj for not taking me
to #1 Station for walking home at night past curfew /
staring through the crosshair
at the lifeguard who lifted me onto a bed
raised like an altar with his wingman watching
after dosing my iced tea with a roofie.

I am breathing hard.
My heart is pounding.
My arm has steadied.
I have cocked the hammer.

My eye is on the target
for all my sisters grabbed and groped /

fingered and beaten / raped and murdered /
who suffer daily affronts and shamings
in offices / on elevators / on trains / in streets
just trying to get home.

I am looking at you
who have dared to say
as a woman tells the truth about her life
that she's just overreacting or hysterical.
I am ready
to press my finger to the metal.

This is no mere metaphor.
This is a life
rife with righteous indignation.
This is a wound
bleeding and pulsing with pain.

Haibun for Crows

Two crows set eyes on me. Flapping, they twitter, rattle, and click unlike yesterday's loosening of brash caws as I first passed under their pine where now a dead one lies belly up with broken wing.

The murder descends, mobbing as if to decide some fate in cackles and chirps. Then as suddenly as they land, they lift off—

> span the open sky
> in thick branches of black sheen
> crisscrossing clear blue.

Emptied

(during the pandemic)

...freedom and happiness are found in the flexibility and ease with which we move through change.—Gautama Buddha

The streets and playgrounds, courts and fields are emptied.
The string of row house rockers emptied of coffee klatches
across porch rails. Silence on cobbles glistening in morning dew,
a heady scent of honeysuckle wafts by windows we peer through.

To escape our solitudes, our ears cock to the sparrow's song.
Sun sets on pyramids, creek beds, ice floes, desert flowers
forging views of the world. Ghosts carouse night winds
of our mourning, all eyes on clear skies boasting stars above

moored cargo ships, snowcapped peaks, the steamy rainforests.
Our windows frame emptied harbors, farmlands and vineyards,
fire escapes and stoops. All of it emptied of the large and small
of singular pleasures in our fractured lives in the godawful air.

Dark Eyes, An Elegy for Ukraine

…whatever I do/will become forever what I've done.
—from "Life While-You-Wait," Wislawa Szymborska

The girl's family gathers at the kitchen table,
her box of colored pencils and pad of paper
that praised the beauty of nightingales in trees
packed away with a book of verse and trident
charm wrapped inside a silky blue-yellow flag.

Potatoes simmer on the stove to mash to stuff
pirohi dough. But now they make molotov cocktails,
fill shell casings, balk at air raid sirens and booms
in a blood red sky bleeding down on stuffed satchels
made ready to cross some border, any border.

The girl's Baba, just outside the window, braves
a soldier, hands him a fistful of sunflower seeds,
implores him to put down his gun to plant them.
While others deliver curses and spells, she sings
"Ochi Chyornye," the street thickening with the fog
of ghosts who have come, who are about to come.

Patchwork Dream Pantoum with Wings

Inside walls of sleep we are singing,
honey throated birds bejeweled
beneath the long sigh of sky, then stilled
we dip and land, our song our banner.

Honey throated birds bejeweled
in the soft light of early morning,
we dip and land, our song our banner,
common wrens trilling in dawn's chorus.

In the soft light of early morning,
hopping along tangles of new branches,
common wrens trilling in dawn's chorus,
we rouse the day fluttering mottled wings.

Hopping along tangles of new branches,
brood stirring within flowering vines,
we rouse the day fluttering mottled wings,
tumble notes into the light and the wind.

Brood stirring within flowering vines
beneath a long sigh of sky, then stilled,
we tumble notes to the light and the wind.
Inside walls of sleep we are singing.

It Is Enough for Now

Villanelle for Mornings

It is enough in this first breath of morning
to lie here with you, light slipping between us,
our fingers laced, lids still swollen with sleep.

Enough to listen to the distant sound of an early train,
song of a buoys in the bay, wind bells in the breeze.
It is enough in this first breath of morning

to talk about the night's dreams, and to dream
across seas, up rivers, into the wild hills,
our fingers laced, lids still swollen with sleep.

It is enough to hold onto each other,
to keep each other still and quiet in place.
It is enough in this first breath of morning,

enough to breathe in the sky, the bright of sun
crossing and washing the continents of our bodies.
It is enough in this first breath of morning,
our fingers laced, lids still swollen with sleep.

III.

...we tumble notes to the light and wind,
dip and land, our song our banner...

Roses at the Coal Drifts

I will tell the truth wherever I please.—Mother Jones

I. Life in Hunky Hollow at the Cost of Coal
   (Windber, Pennsylvania)

Once winter settled across mine patch fields
everyone shivered inside weatherboarded flats,
huddled into each other like house wrens under eaves.
Wood burning cookstoves took the chill from mornings
in Hunky Hollow off Old Scalp Hill, families
carefully crossing newspaper carpeted floorboards
they could never afford to finish in the company house,
nothing like the bossmen's Queen Annes up on the hill
with their wraparound porches, blazing fireplaces,
running water, and indoor bathrooms.

Some afternoons, alive with sun, mothers
scheduled laundry by the way the wind blew in
from the colliery. Kids joined in the dance
of clothes hanging, handing up wooden pins
and folding themselves inside fresh sheets
between the outhouse and the smokehouse
as Eureka No. 40's cars banged feeding the plant,
whine of blowers cleaning bituminous gems,
scent of roses at the coal drifts.

Everything on tick to King Coal grab-all stores,
money moved like water through a bucket
with holes, paycheck deductions washing over
mine owners until debt ran out that never could,

their big barges swollen with coal cars and profits
fueling steel, rail, and electric industries
as soot and ash clawed faces in the mines.

II. Comfort Wives and the System of Esau
    (Beckley, West Virginia)

Mining men liked to tipple and gamble,
get rowdy, while churchwomen were fettered
in silence and fear by The Company Store.
Unlike Old Testament Esau, who relinquished
his birthright for food, their bodies were traded
back of the store in rape rooms to company guards
for a poke of beans, loaf of bread, bottle of milk
to feed children or for one more week's rent
to keep a roof overhead. In the front rooms,
double-dealing company men waited their turn,
as they mastered skulduggery in small-town politics.

They issued scrip to wives to buy things
when husbands couldn't work, collateralized
their flesh to pay off debt, no one daring to say
what went on in Whipple's Shoe Room,
what men dubbed just a bit of hanky-panky
as they gave gift boxes of shoes to women
they sullied, women who often instead rigged
their own from cardboard, newspaper, twine
or chose to go barefoot burying those shoes
in bedroom closets with their shame,
mourning doves cooing at windowsills.

Some as young as twelve were dispatched
along the Appalachians into coalfields
as comfort wives, and if they grew big with child,

their babies pilfered and bartered for rifles or hogs.
Bosses used men and boys in mines
to work rock face chipping, cutting, blasting.
They used women and girls in fields,
across floorboards, mouths silenced with gags
of grief, hope left to roses at the coal drifts,
all their petals laced with black dust.

They Call Me Nellie Bly

I am cold. This madhouse air
clings to my goosebump flesh.
I am tired. They turned me mule,
tethered me to a cart to pull.
I am thirsty. Even for their dirty water.
I am hungry. Even for their rancid meat,
rotted fruit, and moldy bread.

I have wandered tattered, sleepless,
wild-eyed, babbling to get here.
To get choked and beaten,
to lie down upon a soiled bed
all to prove my mettle, to tell
what no man would have me tell,
my pen at his eye should he try
to lift my skirt behind a printing press.

I am Elizabeth Jane Cochrane.
They call me Nellie Bly after the tune
Nelly Bly! Nelly Bly! Bring de broom
along. We'll sweep de kitchen clean,
my dear, And hab a little song.
The broom my pen, newsprint
my voice. I am cold. I am tired.
I thirst and hunger for truth,
the meat and the mettle, my song
Daughters of freedom
arise in your might! March to
the watchwords: Justice and Right!

The Washerwoman

(after Peder Mork Monsted's *Laundry Day* 1905)

The washerwoman's back aches as she hauls
gallons of water to fill tubs to soak, wash, rinse.
She scrubs skirts and shirts on the washboard,
grates a block of soap of ashes lye, and fat
for suds tinged by blue to bleach out
the yellow, her hands scalded red by the steam.

The washerwoman stares from the washtub
through the window as she loses the courtyard view
of children playing at stick ball and skip rope
as she hangs the barrel's wet wash from its line
of hooks, before some make it to the box mangle
to be ironed smooth for those who will dirty them
romping on tennis courts or playing lawn croquet

while the washerwoman fills tub after tub
for the next batch, and the next, and the next.

Walking the Steel

Skywalkers,
the roughnecks
in a tough time
straddled beams
skyscraping steel.

No high wire act
nor Gay 90's applause
for scaffolding snakes
riveting girders in space,
just paydays

with nowhere to go
but to flophouses
with windowless walls
as towers and bridges
and arches rose.

Cowboys of the clouds
in a Gilded Age
erecting steel, believing
only the sky
was the limit.

Unholy Triptych for New Immigrants

Madres—
women forced to spread
their legs and open their mouths
to coyotes in deserts
or inside shipping containers
or hooked to Mack Trucks,
husbands and children
torn from them—
your tired   your poor

Padres—
men in safe houses
along the long route
brave the borders,
starved and beaten,
badgered and bullied,
berated as bad hombres
and drug dealing animals—
yearning   to breathe free

Niños—
child after child dies
in the shallows and the sands
or sweating and shivering
crying themselves to sleep
caged in chain link pens,
garlic tied to their shoes
to ward off the snakes—
no lamp beside   a golden door

Harvest Season

All winemakers should be able to offer something about the grape that is hidden.—Gustavo Bramhila, picker turned vintner

More than its lab tested tannins, sugar, acid levels in the workroom,
more than the swirl, sniff, sip, throwaways in tasting room spittoons,
this journey is of a bracero's gloved hand shearing spurs,
child tugging at a leg of memor, begging "Papa please don't go."

This is the journey walking vineyards to smell and taste the grape
by pickers with headlamps, insects fluttering faces into the night,
more than dumping plastic bins of globes into smoked barrels,
more than the planting and pruning, the washing and pressing.

More than the journey darkened by the ravage of fire and ash,
sunsets blazing across the shadows of vines and everyday lives
in a chiaroscuro of sleek black crows perched on a fence in fog,
more than a smokey cloud feathered sky clearing in the light.

Fire and Water 4th of July

Don't play with matches, I always chided,
a hard rule in the summer of his sixth year.

So that 4th of July morning I took him off to fish
for the first time, hooked the worm to show him
how it's done, went off to fish with this fatherless son,
my only one. I kept an eye on him there, limp rod
in hand, arm propped on knee, chin resting on his fist,
staring aimlessly across the wakeless riverbank
as a line from Elizabeth Bishop rose in me:

while his gills were breathing in the terrible oxygen—
and then I packed everything up and headed home.

He didn't want the water but the fire, a night alight
with sprays of stars we could make come and go,

so I lit an M80. All whoosh, whistle, and bang it skittered
unbridled across the walk, no explosion skyward, instead
a slapdash leap into a tree, not the kind a child could climb,
but parched and spindly. A plume of flame dug in its teeth
of heat crackling branches. Despite a dousing, foliage turned
into a splayed shadow of a thing, smoking limbs pointing
to the moon and artificial stars of constructed constellations.

It was then I thought of Robert Frost's love of a tree:
let there never be curtain drawn between you and me

and pined for what would be the absence of birds, their nesting
and songs, as I pulled my boy inside, lowered the sash and the blind.

Alaskan Haibun

Sailing past Tracy Arm, Juneau

Spruce and hemlock pepper sheared granite cliffs
sculpted by ice age glaciers where waterfalls trickle
and an avalanche rumbles and tumbles down
in crumbling walls of snow in a summer melt,
surface of the fjord dusted brown in sediment,
cracking and popping.

> at water's edge seals
> mount blue rafts, teach pups to swim
> and rest, swim and rest

Two Troves

1. The Mound

Children once scrambled up Indian Mound's bluff
to its dome in Pittsburgh's McKees Rocks Bottoms,
bicycles hastily dropped on their sides at its foot.
They scurried to unearth a trove of arrowheads,
chunks of tortoise shell, stone pottery beads
from the dusty loam of the burial ground, treasures
that hadn't been quarried, robbed, or collected
into Carnegie Museum's cardboard storage chests.

They would tell and retell stories of General McKee,
rumored to have leapt to his death fleeing Indians
he betrayed trading Fort Pitt's smallpox ward
blankets of death for their corn and beans,
tell and retell stories of giants interred there,
ancient aliens, angel brides, superhero shamans,

all while roasting Oscar Meyers on tree branches
shaved with pocketknives over a circle fired
by Blue Tips and Sunday funnies of Bumsteads,
Pluto and Goofy, the Archie crew before returning
the trove back to the dirt and ash, shaking off
all the bad omens and any angry spirits.

2. The Dump

Children scamper and scavenge with pails
and ziplock bags off the Northern California
Coastal Trail in Ft. Bragg's low tide, collect gems

of tossed glass castoffs from drugstore junk
and liquor bottles pitched over the cliff into the sea
along with cars, appliances, anything else fires
could not reduce that could sink into the deep,
into the town dump to be reborn—

washed in on waves as smooth red, blue,
green, brown glittering shards of sea glass
from ruby taillights, sapphire apothecary jars,
amber beer bottles, all awash with sea foam,
pounded and tossed in mermaid swells
to become something else, to become

earrings and bracelets wrapped in filigree,
encased pendants dangling from chains,
epoxied mosaic sun catchers, all rising up
from an underwater garden to pricey Mendocino
market stands, shops, and galleries. Deserted
seaside memories collected with troves
of shells and driftwood dumped yet again,
this time at the bottom of guesthouse drawers.

What a Doll!

Barbie was everything we didn't want to be…everything
the feminist movement was trying to escape.—Gloria Steinem

They keep hawking her,
the busty Barbie
with wasp waist
and tiny feet,
original bachelor party
gag gift in lingerie
and peek-a-boo box.

They keep pushing her
inside the Dream House,
inside a body the dream
for a future to travel
bare and smooth, a passport
of boobs and buttocks.

They keep propping her up
as rockstar, reporter, pilot,
engineer (of washing machines),
tech head computing code
(for drawing puppies),
even Barbie for President
(gowned and bejeweled).

What a hustle the token
blue-collar and blackface Barbie
carpenter, firefighter, nurse,
dentist and all donning careers

like new hats, sporting tights and spikes
and always fashion forward.

What a hype this dolly
for fixing bodies by starving,
waxing, plumping, binding,
and slicing—this Barbie,
in all the wrong proportions
in too many ways to measure.

Negative Pleasure

This is a poem that bumps into you
in the dark, doesn't excuse itself,
makes you want to dust yourself off,
straighten up, move along as if
nothing ever happened. This poem
offers no apology for the discomfort
it causes, continues to stumble drunken
on its own discontent, lumbers along
all the jagged edges, unsettling under
thunderous skies, leaden footed
sinking into quicksand with teeth.
This poem has lost its place. This poem
is reductive. It is nothing. It is lost, locked
in a room without windows or doors.

Circling the Tables

We have circled so many tables topped
by formica or wood, marble or glass,
with mugs of tea, plates of fortune cookies,
espresso and chocolate, the wine and biscotti,
baguettes and cheese—spreading, crunching,
filling up on our tireless conversations
and grand opinions on the state of things
spilling freely across their surfaces.

Then there was all that backyard fence talk
about the woman who cries every Saturday night,
that wayward girl who ran off with the local
bad boy and his guitar on a Harley, a man
with Alzheimer's who turned fire starter,
talk about whatever wasn't as we'd like it—
too much war, not enough money, all of us
growing wider and grayer than expected.

How often we squeezed in around those tables
in small kitchens or long stretches of dining rooms,
as if our heart-to-hearts would solve it all,
transform our worlds. Today I find myself
quiet and alone, hungry for a feast of table talk,
dreaming us all back again, chewing over
breaking news and fearlessly writing recipes
for all our protests, actions, revolutions,
and living it up, like it really mattered.

Saturday's Child

She'll never sell out/She never will/
Not for a dollar bill.—Donna Summer

As Saturday's child, I did have to work hard for the money:
Cataloging the sale and return of department store garb
after being transferred for not being what the boss called
his "hot tomato," promotion dangled as a shared room
on a business trip, and for the first time learning to say no.

Pulling on a fringed bikini and knee high boots to jump
from a bull rope onto a stage as a beachside go-go girl,
even after failing a bare-breasted audition. Cranking out
fish lures and offered pay under the table as the supervisor's
"pretty little bird to train," then flipping him off in a walkout.

Getting stiffed on tips waiting corporate parties, sweating out
mid-summer short orders of cheesy omelettes and fluffy pancakes
washed down with pitchers of Bloody Marys and Mimosas.
Grabbed by the throat by a drunken pill-popping veteran
for shutting him off from another Long Island Iced Tea.

Editing grad students' theses on just a high school education,
chasing them down for their chump change and rubber checks.
Proofreading briefs and blindsided by hands at the back, waist,
hips, thighs. Dropping out of a PhD program after A's turned B's
for standing up the professor advisor at the local literary pub.

Teaching a boy to understand magnetism and constellations
who would go braindead quarterbacking, another to read
who would end up a ward of court for crawling through
windows to open doors for her strung-out burglar father.

Propositioned by the school's superintendent, quitting that job.

And, as the fortune telling rhyme goes: Monday's child may be
fair of face, Tuesday's full of grace, Wednesday's with its woes,
Thursday's having far to go, Friday's loving and giving,
Sunday's bonny and blithe, but this Saturday's child
really had to work hard for a living, in more ways than one

I don't get periods, just exclamation points!

Becoming a woman was explained to so many of us
in clichés, the couched innuendos, and silences.
Instructions for me arrived in the Kotex Corporation
boxed pamphlet, "You're a Young Lady Now."

Inside the carton under a soft pink cover appeared
a sanitary napkin with elastic belt and clips
that would bring chafing, pinching, welts, wedgies,
feeling frumpy with a wad of cotton in the pants.

Even after moving on to disposable tampons,
washable sea sponges, eco-friendly cloth pads,
and heightened awareness, women curl up bloated
in bed when the curse of cramps knocks at the door.

We are still chastised by words: being on the rag,
told to take a pill, to stop being so moody
or oh so touchy, far too sensitive, overreactive
as Aunt Flo sails in to visit on the crimson wave.

German women hear about the Code Red Alarm,
the French get a crime scene in their panties,
Chinese a Bloody Mary, Russians the Red Army.
I tell sisters now how to silence common aspersions:

Hang from your door, desk, computer screen a sign:
"I have PMS and a handgun. Now just walk away!"

Rodeo Rondel

Horses will be made to look as wild as their cowboys are brave
beneath a big top carnival sky, all boughs of cotton candy clouds
inside a gun smoke dome, above a scrappy yawn of land between
the palms and pines, farms of wind on the rise in rodeo country.

Ruddy-faced caballeros sporting ten-gallon hats, buckles, and spurs
race the road a hum and blur of cars under dawn's watercolor sky.
Horses will be made to look as wild as their cowboys are brave.

Unbridled broncos only paw at dry brush, pasture veined in ruts.

Horses nuzzle at roadside posts before their flanks are strapped
and lassos snap necks back at a slaughterhouse stop off, foothills
a surge of flags and flashes in a brazen hoopla in rodeo country
where horse are made to look as wild as their cowboys are brave.

Belled Doe

—for all the innocents

At first light, the white-tailed doe
trots straight across the wooded acre
past the neighbor's weathered cabin
and blaze-orange vest drying on a hook,
trots right up to our breakfast nook window.

Morning after morning, the doe returns
for a hand-fed Winesap after foraging,
salt lick on its way from the mercantile
in the hope she might turn bellwether
for her own fawns. For now, safely belled,

she sports a florescent orange ribbon
embroidered with dangling peace symbol
talisman against incoming hunting season.
Yet this doe still ends up with its hind legs
roped and slung from a line, strung up

between two hearty oaks, their leaves
not yet red for fall, shell casings a hunter
kissed for luck scattered on the ground,
militia flag draping his muzzleloader
propped against the whitewashed wall.

Brass bell tinkling in the rising breeze,
its baubles of dew glistening in breaking day
drip down into a blue bucket under her head,
catching the last low groan of her death moan.

Lion Dance Haibun for Won Kee

Won Kee Supermarket flings open its doors to a lion of bamboo,
paper, and cloth. It dances with sparks of firecrackers, bang
of drums, clash of cymbals, wards off evil and brings good fortune
blinking its eyes, hungry mouth open for gifts of greens.

> indoors bright red bows
> lilies and sweet plum blossoms
> grace the bowl

Irregular Pulse Beat Sonnet

To every politician taking donations from the NRA, shame on you.
—Emma Gonzalez, school shooting survivor.

The relentless drone of the daily news
sends the pulse racing as homes that swelled
with laughter weep from joists and beams,
sun-washed rooms darkened by drawn curtains.

In days of the dead, the gunmen cackled
loading, reloading, riveting body after body
already downed, bullet after bullet after bullet.
Bodies halted on a nightclub dance floor,

bodies layered one upon the other under desks,
bodies in seats, eyes locked on a fuzzy movie screen,
bodies at tables, fingers frozen coloring butterflies,
bodies halted at prayer with those of us

who survive, stay alive. Hearts aching,
our own bodies pulse
                    and pulse
                            and breathe.

Kamloops Shoes Pantoum

The voices of ancestors are smothered in sleep
where footless shoes climb steps in memoriam,
215 pairs of shoes enshrined for schoolchildren,
their First Nation's presence preserved.

Where footless shoes climb steps in memoriam
beneath the wingspan of the golden-eyed eagle.
Their First Nation's presence is preserved
by invisible feet in little shoes that pace a legacy

beneath the wingspan of the golden-eyed eagle
soaring and hovering over a mass grave.
Invisible feet in little shoes pace a legacy
in the hoo hoo hoot of owls in the wind

soaring and hovering over a mass grave,
shapeshifting mountain lion prowling grounds
in the hoo hoo hoot of owls in the wind
as wandering ghosts torn from their tribes.

Shapeshifting mountain lion prowling grounds,
215 pairs of shoes enshrined for schoolchildren,
wandering ghosts are torn from their tribes,
the voices of ancestors smothered in sleep.

Temples

...oh God of mercy, oh wild God.
—from Gerald Stern's "The Dancing"

Holy temple in the Sinai fallen,
Sacred Mosque in Mosul desecrated,
pagan temples of Alexandria downed,
Hindu temples leveled by fire,
Buddhist statues shattered,
Guyana temple poisoned.

> One more racial warrior
> heeds coded whistle calls
> from the storm front
> in the White House
> in the language of fear.

> One more fist flung high,
> flags heaved and flaunted
> before burning crosses.
> Pittsburgh Tree of Life Synagogue
> a massacre of the reverent.

Churches ablaze in St. Landry Parish,
houses of worship riddled by bullets
from Escondido to New Zealand.
Temples invaded and defiled
in splatters of human blood.
Temples toppled by hate, and then
one more, one more, one more—
> Oh, God. Oh wild God,
> have mercy.

Haibun at Dusk at Water's Edge

Sailboats slide into their docks for the night. Droopy lidded
curtains cross windows. The music of a party yacht boasts
its entry, dog onboard a nearby slip barking and howling.
The neighbor's cats corral and screech, ruffle bushy blossoms
of marigolds perfuming dusk.

> a peachy sky turns
> weighty slate of gray, grieving
> sunken corpses in rough channels

A continent away, cities darken and public places empty.
Sidewalks littered with shattered glass and broken hearts
remain in vigil along streets of the dead and wounded,
laughter and conversation buried beneath night covers
where lovers should turn and touch and talk.

> we tip wine glasses
> to sky, toast the moon's craters,
> its smile turned downward

Beached

Low tide whispers
his name as sun sets down
as seabirds ruffle
golden braids of light

cross the water's sheen
then nose up away
into a cloudless sky
here

where the water's mouth
swallowed a man whole
from the seabed floor

where

he gasped and choked
on his own sobs
here
where

I trace names
in the sand
of all my dead
pray

whether death chose him
or he chose death
the water will cradle him
in boundless arms.

Haibun in Another Fire Season

The smell of ash wakes me in my bed, burning
my nostrils and throat, midnight, as I dream
of water webbed lashes and a cool, damp face.

Diablo winds sling fiery plumes all night across
grapevines, redwoods, schoolhouses, ranches,
livestock and wildlife left behind, everything
trying to catch its breath.

In the gloom of gray hours before dawn, I write
words without paper or pen in a half-awake state
while winds whistle and howl across the dock,
through the trees, my open window, and this poem

> stumbling ahead
> as new dawn struggles to breathe
> tears blurring the skies.

She'd Sit and Sew

A curious gladness shook me.—Stanley Kunitz

Evenings she'd sit there rocking and sewing,
darning a sock, stitching a tattered buttonhole,
hemming a skirt, or the more elaborate projects
crocheting a hat, shawl, or throw as if this

private piece work were its own peace.
Even as repetition weakened her weary hands,
she sometimes reached down to tousle my hair
as I slumped in a sleepy heap at her feet,

and when through the dusty blind slats
a thin thread of light streaked across my lap,
it was then that curious gladness shook me.

Drifting Zuihitsu

Dreams carry me to barren stretches of concrete peppered by buttons of stone beyond the stars on a precipice from which to view the world.

Everything couples in greens and browns. Walks are long and steady with no field of vision for what came before, what is to follow.

Curtains are drawn, doors latched. There is no entrance, no welcome.

I inhale the sky, it's blues and whites, its silences. *It is not the voice that commands the story: it is the ear.*

Breezy jazz off a ragged skiff drifts along the lick of water to its boat in the berth, bat ray nearing its barnacled bow.

I squint in the bright summer sun, doze wrapped in a warm cloak of air.

Foggy silhouettes of my dead in cruciform tiptoe through, shushing each other, knowing I am sure to shoo them off.

Wind chimes dance and slide their cymbals up against each other. Dark flocks of geese squawk inside the beat of their wide wings.

My time to fly has yet to be born in me.

Not much, just everything

the way the heart of a house throbs
with soup bubbling on the stove
rich with the garden's best

the way it bathes in the light
of a super moon or feasts on stars
in a bowl of clouds

the way wild geese stir its silence
on a tongue of wind and wingbeats
sweeping across the sky

the way we rest our flesh in it
with full bellies and fish mouths
swimming inside sleep

the way dreamy reveries drift in and out
on currents and waves of first light
singing the day's blessings

the way the finch and dove do
above dissipating low flung fog
in a sun kissed morning

fragrant with dewy sage and mint
and then and then and then
not much, just everything

She, sister who reads this poem

*...I know you are reading this poem because there is nothing else
left to read/there where you have landed...*—Adrienne Rich

I imagine you standing at the stove on a breathy night
before an open window, breeze flirting crisp kitchen curtains,
one hand at the hip, the other stirring soup, tasting, adding
a bit of basil and lemon thyme. Imagine you musing about
this poem as it quiets like a child off in the next room into
something. Something taking your attention, startling, stirring
outside the lines of unshorn weeds choking flowering sage
you will get to once you finish reading this poem again, rising
perhaps from bed, words blurring your eyes in a half-awake state,
some foggy mess of meaning you chase after and cannot catch.

I imagine you, she who reads this poem, stirring toward
the day unfolding ahead, alone and unafraid, surefooted
along a sandy beach, its sandcastles, seashells, tossed limbs
and bulbs of seaweed tangling your feet, all part of the poem.
Imagine another woman, the invisible one pushing a broom
through a dusk lit hall, poem in the pocket of her cleaning cart
folded behind disinfectant spray. And the borrowed woman,
poem tucked at the back of a stroller rolled out to the walk,
reading this poem at water's edge, arms flung wide to morning.

I imagine you, sister who reads this poem, braving a ridge line
along a blustery bay on your own, poem rummaged from inside
an old backpack at night's campfire then carted carefully off
to the dimly lit pup tent like a child finally quieted, her belly full
of hobo stew and s'mores. Or like a wind so soft it passes

barely noticed across a piney wood, I imagine you, sister
who reads this poem, barely stirring yet part of the poem,
its fire and its flame.

Author's Notes

"All the Ways I Do Not Want to Die"
Quoted matter is from Lawrence Ferlinghetti's "The World Is A Beautiful Place"and Mary Oliver's "When Death Comes." The Chilean poet noted is Pablo Neruda.

"Anchorless in the Light"
The title and phrase are from "The Changing Light" by Lawrence Ferlinghetti.

"Born Under the Influence Dämmerschlaf Pantoum"
Scopolamine-morphine, used into the 1960's, induced amnesia, delirium, postpartum depression, infant central nervous system weakening necessitating slapping of the bottom to stimulate breathing. Dämmerschlaf, German for painless childbirth, was called Twilight Sleep.

"Broken Pitcher"
Bouguereau, from a wine and olive oil merchant family, his paintings often focused on young girls and loss of innocence appealing to wealthy patrons..

"Column of Strength Comfort Station"
Comfort women were sex slaves from Korea, China, other occupied countries for the WWII Japanese Army. Kim Hak-Sun first spoke out as a comfort woman. "Corporate Goddesses" wraithlike statues ring the building behind the sculpture.

"Crossing Boundaries"
La Belle Equipe, run by a Muslim-Jewish couple, was one of the 2015 café terrorist attacks.

"Dark Eyes, An Elegy for Ukraine"
The nightingale is Ukraine's national bird said to sing songs of
cheer, trident an emblem of independence, sunflower a national
symbol of peace. "Ochi Chyornye" or "Dark Eyes," often seen as a
Russian-Romani song, was written by Ukrainian poet Yevhen
Hrebinda.

"Drifting Zuihitsu"
The ancient Japanese form"follows the brush" or "drifts like clouds"
in loosely connected poetry and prose responding to surroundings.
Quoted matter is from Italo Calvino.

"Fire and Water 4th of July"
Quoted lines are from Elizabeth Bishop's "The Fish" and Robert
Frost's "Tree at My Window."

"I didn't want him to see me"
Catholic leaders covered up PA priests' sexual abuse of over a
thousand children. On statues noted: St. Agnes was executed for
refusing to marry a Roman official. Magdalen, said to have self-
exiled to the desert to atone for prostitution, which some believe
retaliation for being Christ's favorite disciple. The priest in this
poem ran off with the local high school's valedictorian.

"Kamloops Shoes Pantoum"
Artist Tamara Bell placed shoes on Vancouver Art Gallery steps to
memorialize 215 school ground remains in a mass grave at Canada's
Kamloops Indian Residential School federal project for European
assimilation. Thousands have since been unearthed.

"Landay for the Woman on the Floor"
The Landay's nine and thirteen syllabic couplet form was invented
for collective and anonymous authorship of uncomfortable subjects
by Pashtun women who lacked freedom of speech.

"Ravensbrück Pantoum"
Ravensbrück concentration camp enslaved, murdered, medically experimented upon women.

"Rodeo Rondel"
This is a Frank O'Hara style rondel with floating line and abandoned rhyme.

"She, the one you call sister"
This cento uses first lines from Adrienne Rich books in this order: *Snapshots of a Daughter-in-Law*, *Leaflets*, *Diving into the Wreck*, *The Dream of a Common Language*, *A Wild Patience Has Taken Me This Far*, *The Atlas of a Difficult World*, *Dark Fields of the Republic*, *Tonight No Poetry Will Serve*.

"She, the one who is my songbird"
Cherita is a linked form of one, two, three line stanzas. *Pajarilla* is a bird; *mi amor* my love, *querida mia* my dear, *cantadora* singer, *joropo* folk dance, *para toda la vida* forever after, *tú eres* you are.

"The milkman's daughter"
To refer to a child as the milkman's daughter implied adultery at a time when housebound women had limited access to men other than their husbands.

"They Call Me Nelly Bly"
19 C Nelly Bly, first female investigative reporter, became an inmate at the Women's Lunatic Asylum on New York'a Blackwell Island to expose conditions. Lyrics are from Steven Foster's "Nelly Bly" (1850) and George Cooper's "Daughters of Freedom, The Ballot Be Yours" (1871).

"Two Troves"
Indian Mound dates back over 2,000 years to the Adena people; the Seneca are relocating its artifacts to an educational site in McKees Rocks, PA. The Dump, or Glass Beach, is part of Mac Kerricher State Park in Ft. Bragg, CA where glass removal is a misdemeanor.

"Unholy Triptych for New Immigrants"
Stanza last lines are from Emma Lazarus' "New Colossus" on the Statue of Liberty.

"Walking the Steel"
The International Workers Association, founded in Pittsburgh, "The City of Bridges," unionized Iron Workers. The higher the climb, the higher the wage.

"What a Doll"
Ruth Handler patterned Barbie in 1959 after German tabloid cartoon, Lilli, an underdressed blonde bombshell working girl who became a hitchhiking dashboard bobblehead. Handler said she wanted a doll with breasts so girls could see their future.

Acknowledgements

The author is grateful to these print periodicals and anthologies for including these poems as first publications or reprints, sometimes in earlier versions:

Artemis Journal: "Ravensbrück Pantoum" (2019), "Imperfect Contrition" (2020)
Aurorean: "Alaskan Haibun" (2019)
Autumn Sky Poetry Daily: "Dancing Zuihitsu" (2020)
A Walk with Nature Anthology: "Haibun for Crows" (2019)
Bacopa Literary Magazine: "This Is to Say" (2020)
Blue Collar Review Journal of Progressive Working Class Literature: "Irregular Pulse Beat Sonnet," "Walking the Steel" (2018), "Roses at the Coal Drifts" (2019)
Bryant Literary Review: "Living Dolls" (2019)
Caesura Literary Magazine: "Belled Doe" (2018), "Dreamers" (2021)
California Quarterly: "Patchwork Dream Pantoum with Wings," "It Is Enough for Now Villanelle for Mornings" (2019)
Cider Press Review Journal of Contemporary Poetry: "She, sister who reads this poem" (2020)
Coneflower Cafe: "Two Troves" (2022)
Conestoga Zen Anthology: "At Pine Cove," "Dreaming Zuihitsu," "Fire and Water 4th of July" (2021)
Connecticut River Review: "Harvest Season" (2021)
Copper Nickel: "Rodeo Rondel" (2005)
Delmarva Review: "Anchorless in the Light," "Circling the Tables," "I didn't want him to see me," "Self-portrait, out of focus" (2019)
Ethel: "Dreamers" (2022)
Gold Man Review: "Sonnet Spooning" (2020)
Gyroscope Review: "Landay for the Woman on the Floor" (2019)

Haight Ashbury Literary Review: "Kamloops Shoes Pantoum" (2022)

I Don't Cry Anymore Anthology: "Wounds That Bleed Inside," "This Is to Say" (2022)

Isacoustics iii: "At Pine Cove," "Haibun for Crows" (2018)

Last Stanza Poetry Journal: "Saturday's Child," "Driving from Pescadero" (2021)

Light on the Walls of Life Lawrence Ferlinghetti Tribute Anthology: "Anchorless in the Light" (2022)

Maintenant Journal of Contemporary Dada Writing and Art: "Play" (2020); "Two Troves" (2022)

Missing Persons Reflections on Dementia Anthology: "The Way It Is" (2019)

Motherscope, A Collection of Birth Stories: "Born Under the Influence (2019)

North Dakota Quarterly: "Another Birth Story" (2020)

Overthrowing Capitalism, World Without Wars: "Cinderman" (2019), "Femicide" (2021)

Penumbra Literary and Art Journal: "Blue Suitcase," "Negative Pleasure" (2021)

Pittsburgh Post Gazette: "They Call Me Nelly Bly" (2019)

Plainsongs 40/2: "Summer Haibun" (2020)

Poems-for-All: "Dark Eyes," "Unholy Triptych for New Immigrants" (2022)

Raven Chronicles Journal 25: "I've got my finger on the trigger, too" (2018)

Santa Fe Review: "I remember when I was just a kid" (2019)

Shanghai Literary Review: "Born Under the Influence" (2019)

South Dakota Review: "Not much, just everything," "Production Lines" (2021)

Storms of the Inland Sea: Poems of Alzheimer's & Dementia Caregiving Anthology: "The Way It Is" (2021)

Sutterville Review: "The milkman's daughter" (2021)

Switchgrass Review: "Broken Pitcher" (2022)

Together Behind Four Walls Anthology: "Emptied" (2021)
Toyon Literary Review Movement Issue: "Crossing Boundaries" (2019)
Xinachtli Journal: "Kamloops Shoes Pantoum" (2022)

The author also thanks these online sites for first printing or
    reprinting these poems:
Autumn Sky Poetry Daily: "Dancing Zuihitsu" (2020)
Boston Literary Magazine: "Mailbox" (2020)
Buddhist Poetry Review: "Summer Haibun," "Dancing Zuihitsu,"
    "Beached" (2020)
Caesura Literary Magazine: Open Skate" (2018)
Cloud Women's Quarterly Journal: "Triolet for Spring," "Summer
    Haibun," "She, sister who reads this poem" (2021)
Digital Paper: "Anchorless in the Light," "Summer Haibun" (2021)
Humble Pie: "She, the one you call sister" (2021)
International Human Rights Arts Festival: "Crossing Boundaries"
    (2021)
Lothlorien Poetry Journal: "She Sit and Sew," "What a Doll!" "She,
    the queen bee marries winter," "All the Ways I Do Not Wish to
    Die" (2021)
Marsh Hawk Review: "Born Under the Influence" (2020)
Monterey Poetry Review: "It is Enough for Now Villanelle for
    Mornings" (2019); "Beached," "Drifting Zuihitsu" (2020);
    "Dreamers," "Harvest Season," "Patchwork Dream Pantoum
    with Wings" (2023
New Verse News: "Haibun for Another Fire Season" (2019),
    "Emptied" (2020)
Non Binary Review: "Walking the Steel" (2021)
Nzuri Journal: "Cinderman," "O Brother," "Temptation" (2021)
Revolution (Relaunch): "Unholy Triptych for the New Immigrants"
    (2019), "Femicide" (2020)
Rise Up Review: "She, the one you call sister" (2021)

San Francisco Public Library Poem-of-the-Day: "Broken Pitcher"
(2020)

Still, the Journal: "Temples" (2019)

Ukraine: Light in the Darkness Anthology: "Dark Eyes," "Dreaming
Zuihitsu" 2022

What Rough Beast: "Wounds that Bleed Inside" (2020)

Writing in a Woman's Voice: "At Pine Cove," "I don't get periods. I
get exclamation points," I've got my finger on the trigger, too"
(2018)

Your Daily Poem: "Meditation at the Dunes of Asilomar" (2018),
"Driving from Pescadero" (2020)

The author especially appreciates these publications for honoring
these poems:

*Blue Collar Review Journal of Progressive Working Class
Literature:* Working People's Poetry Competition Honors for
"Roses at the Coal Drifts" (2019)

International Human Rights Arts Festival: Honors for "Crossing
Boundaries" (2020)

Origami Poems Project: Pushcart Prize Nomination for "Triolet for
Spring" (2019)

Poetry Super Highway: Summer Poetry Contest Finalist for
"Dancing Zuihitsu" (2020)

Shanghai Literary Review: Pushcart Prize Nomination for "Born
Under the Influence" (2019)

Ventura County Poetry Project: First Prize for "Born Under the
Influence" (2020)

About the Author and Her Work

Andrena Zawinski is the author of three other poetry books, several chapbooks, and has edited two anthologies. Her poetry has received accolades for free verse, form, lyricism, spirituality, social concern and include a PEN Oakland Josephine Miles Award, Kenneth Patchen Poetry Prize, Emily Stauffer Poetry Prize, *Tiferet* Carriage House Poetry Prize, *Pittsburgh Magazine* Harry Schwalb inaugural Excellence in the Arts Award, Akron Art Museum Prize, *Paterson Literary Review* Allen Ginsberg Honors, and many more with several Pushcart Prize nominations. Her poems have received praise from Lynn Emanuel, Jim Daniels, Len Roberts, Carolyn Wright, Lynne Knight, Jan Beatty, Rebecca Foust, and others for their embrace of the human condition with compassion and intelligence with an unflinching attention to craft.

Born and raised in Pittsburgh, PA as the daughter and granddaughter of steelworkers and coalminers, she earned degrees from the University of Pittsburgh and went on to become a teacher of writing in public school, university, and community college systems as well as a poet-in-residence for educational, arts, and community organizations in Pennsylvania and California. Those included Pittsburgh Public Schools, West Mifflin Schools, Gilmary Therapeutic Treatment Center for Adjudicated Delinquents, Allegheny Community College, University of Pittsburgh, St. Mary's College of California, Peralta Community Colleges, Pittsburgh Council for the Arts, Western Pennsylvania Writing Project, International Poetry Forum, and others. She has also done government, legal, retail, and restaurant work, much of it as a single parent. Zawinski lives in the San Francisco Bay area where as an activist poet and feminist she founded and runs a popular Women's Poetry Salon. She was also longstanding Features Editor at PoetryMagazine.com.

Full Collections:

Landings (2017): 95 pages, Kelsay Books Aldrich Press, Hemet, CA

Something About (2009): 89 pages, Blue Light Press, San Francisco, CA—a 2010 PEN Oakland Josephine Miles Award for Excellence in Literature selected by its president Floyd Salas

Traveling in Reflected Light (1995): 139 pages, Pig Iron Press, Youngstown, Ohio—a Kenneth Patchen Prize in Poetry selected by Joel Climenhaga

Plumes & other flights of fancy in flash fiction, (2022): 70 pages, Writing Knights Press, Cleveland, Ohio

Small Collections:

She (2021), *Drifting Sands* (2019), *Blood Moon & Other Haibun* (2018): micro-chapbooks, Origami Poems Project, Naragansett, RI

Taking the Road Where It Leads (2008): 25 pages, Poets Corner Press, Stockton, CA

Andrena Zawinski's Greatest Hits 1991-2001 (2002): 32 pages, Pudding House, Johnstown, OH

Elegies for My Mother (1999): 19 pages, *The Pittsburgh Quarterly* online Pittsburgh, PA

Poems from a Teacher's Desk: 15 pages and *Six Pack Poems-to-Go* postcard collection (1994): Harris Publications, Carnegie, PA

Anthologies Edited:

Editor: *Turning a Train of Thought Upside Down: An Anthology of Women's Poetry* (2012): 100 pages, Scarlet Tanager Books, Oakland, CA

Co-Editor: *Writing on the Desk: Poems and Prose by Teachers of the Western Pennsylvania Writing Project* (1994): 165 pages, University of Pittsburgh, Pittsburgh, PA